THE SEINE

written and photographed by

Julia Waterlow

Wayland

THE WORLD'S RIVERS

The Amazon
The Danube
The Ganges
The Mississippi
The Nile
The Rhine
The St Lawrence
The Seine
The Thames
The Volga
The Yellow River
The Zaire

Cover *A tourist boat passes the Cathedral of Notre Dame, which was built on an island in the Seine at Paris.*

Series and book editor Rosemary Ashley
Series designer Derek Lee
Book designer Paul Bennett

First published in 1993 by
Wayland (Publishers) Limited
61 Western Road, Hove
East Sussex, BN3 1JD, England

British Library Cataloguing in Publication Data
Waterlow, Julia
The Seine.—(World's Rivers Series)
I. Title   II. Series
914.4

ISBN 0-7502-0771-X

Typeset in the UK by
Dorchester Typesetting Group Ltd
Printed in Italy by G. Canale C.S.p.A.

CONTENTS

1. **THE TWISTING GODDESS**
4

2. **THE RIVER AND ITS LANDSCAPE**
6
The Upper Seine – small beginnings
6
The heart of the Seine – Île de France
8
The Lower Seine – a meandering finish
10
Farming in the Lower Seine
12

3. **HIGHWAY OF FRANCE**
14
Modern river traffic
15
Making the Seine navigable
19
Crossing the River
21

4. THE SEINE IN HISTORY
22
Celts to Vikings
22
Vikings and Normans
25
France as one country
26

5. PARIS
27
The famous waterfront
27
A growing city
30

6. SETTLEMENTS AND INDUSTRY
31
Rouen
31
Le Havre
32
Troyes
34
Other industries of the Seine valley
35

7. ART AND CULTURE
37

8. PLEASURES OF THE SEINE
40
Food and drink
40
Leisure on the Seine
42

9. LOOKING TO THE FUTURE
44
Water control
44
Pollution problems
44
Different demands
45

GLOSSARY
46

BOOKS TO READ AND FURTHER INFORMATION
47

INDEX
48

1. THE TWISTING GODDESS

It is said that the River Seine gets its name from a Roman goddess called Sequana, who was worshipped at the river's source over two thousand years ago. The Roman name Sequana comes from an older Celtic word 'squan', meaning snakelike. The name fits, for few other rivers twist and turn as much as the Seine on its journey to the sea.

Beginning in eastern France, the Seine flows calmly north-westwards, coiling through the rich farmland of northern France and, 776 km from its source, out into the English Channel. About midway along it lies one of the great capital cities of the world, Paris.

Although the Seine is one of the world's shorter rivers, it is an important European waterway. There are few natural obstacles such as waterfalls or rapids that would make navigation difficult for boats; it also serves as the gateway for water-borne traffic from the Atlantic Ocean through to Paris and the city's surrounding industrial areas. As the river narrows upstream, a web of canals takes over and provides routes for barges right to the heart of Europe.

The Seine is also a river of kings and queens; during its long history it has not only known pre-Roman rulers but also Vikings and later the lavish lifestyles of the French royalty. Up and down its length, from source to estuary, castles were built and battles were fought. From the Middle Ages onwards stonemasons worked on elaborate and splendid cathedrals and churches, creating some of the most famous buildings of France.

France is a country which prides itself on its love of culture and pleasure and the Seine valley is no exception. The clear light and reflections of the still river and its tributaries inspired artists and writers, its lush farmland to this day provides rich and mouth-watering food and its waters are enjoyed by people for sport and relaxation.

The Seine, overlooked by the ruins of Chateau Gaillard, winds gently past white chalk cliffs. The castle was planned by King Richard I of England in 1196, at a time when both England and France were fighting each other for control of Normandy.

2. THE RIVER AND ITS LANDSCAPE

Surrounded by leafy woods, small springs collect in a pool that marks the spot where the Seine rises, among the low hills of Burgundy.

The Upper Seine – small beginnings

The source of the Seine lies in a sheltered valley not far from the village of St-Seine-l'Abbaye in Burgundy. Springs feed a pool of water surrounded by trees and from it flows a trickle of water, the young river Seine. It is now a quiet spot but once pilgrims flocked here to worship the goddess Sequana.

Just a stream, the Seine flows off the low hills where it rises and down a small steep valley with wooded sides. It wriggles through meadows grazed by cows, passing mills that once used water power for grinding corn. The town of Châtillon-sur-Seine (which means Châtillon-on-Seine) gives its name to the Châtillon cows found in the area which produce rich milk and cream.

Vineyards of the Champagne region surround the Seine. The grapes are used to make the famous drink, champagne.

Before the river reaches Troyes, it passes through rolling country with chalky limestone soil. Grapes grown on the surrounding hills are used to make the world-famous drink, champagne. Here the Seine is shallow and clear, widening as tributaries begin to join the main flow.

The countryside around and beyond Troyes is flat and open, with few fences or hedges. Roads run straight across the plain and tall poplars line many roads. It is a busy farming area where wheat and sugar beet are grown. Flour mills and sugar refineries lie on the edges of towns.

The first major tributary, the Aube, joins the Seine and the junction marks the highest point that barges can reach. Downstream from here the river is large enough to take commercial boats.

Source of the Seine
In the wood where the Seine rises, is a statue of the goddess Sequana, built by the city of Paris in 1867 to honour the river that is its lifeblood. Nearby are the much older remains of a Roman temple where offerings were made to the goddess. The Romans built baths here too and pilgrims came from all over Europe, believing that the water of the Seine had healing powers. It is thought that the place was probably a very ancient site of worship, long before the Romans arrived.

A watermill beside the Upper Seine, not far from the river's source. Watermills, powered by fast-flowing river water, were once used to grind corn.

The heart of the Seine – Île de France

The area stretching either side of Paris is known as the Île de France. The Seine flows right through the middle and is joined by the rivers Yonne, Loing, Marne and Oise.

The flat land and large fields suit modern farm machinery and the Île de France is one of the most productive farming areas in France. Wheat and sugar beet are two of the main crops as well as oil-seed rape (which blooms in fields of bright yellow flowers), market gardening to supply the people of Paris, and dairy farming. Sugar beet is Europe's main source of sugar and northern France is one of the most important growing areas.

A special feature of the Seine valley either side of Paris is the large amount of woodland that still grows beside the river. Forests like the one at Fontainebleau which extends to 25,000 hectares, have never been cut down (most of northern Europe was once covered by woodland). The forests are carefully managed and replanted when necessary with a variety of different trees such as oaks, ashes, beeches, sycamores, chestnuts and poplars.

The middle stretch of the Seine's journey is through the built up area of Paris, passing houses and factories on the outskirts before reaching the famous waterfront in the city centre. As the river leaves Paris the industrial suburbs sprawl even more densely on either side. Beyond, countryside takes over again and the riverbanks are lined with the lawns and weekend retreats of wealthy Parisians. The river arrives in Normandy.

Left *The Forest of Fontainebleau covers a huge area along the banks of the Seine in the Île de France. This beautiful region is enjoyed by walkers and riders.*

Right *Stone embankments with tree-lined walks guide the river through the centre of Paris.*

The Lower Seine – a meandering finish

The Seine drops only 470 m from its source to the sea (compare this with the Amazon River, which falls 5,250 m!) and most of this fall occurs when the river is young and still small. There are no mountains to make it surge wildly in the spring after winter snow thaws and its tributaries are all equally gentle. Even where it reaches its full width at Rouen the Seine only flows at 500 m³/sec (compared with the River Danube which flows at 9,000 m³/sec). As a result it is not a rushing or powerful river and for most of its length it meanders slowly.

The Lower Seine, the part of the river downstream of Paris and the Île de France, has particularly large meanders because the Seine, like all rivers, slows even more as it gets closer to sea-level. It winds through chalky countryside, swinging from north to south, cutting into cliffs on one side and then depositing the scoured out chalk on the inside of the next bend as silt. The insides of the bends are fertile and flat, ideal for farming.

Amfreville is an important point on the Lower Seine, because the Poses Dam has been built across the river. For the next 200 km downstream to the sea, the river is tidal, rising and falling daily. As the tides come in, the river looks odd since it appears to be flowing the wrong way. Upstream, the river is protected from these changes. Huge locks beside the dam allow river traffic through.

Normandy cows are mainly bred for their milk. They always have dark brown patches around the eyes like spectacles.

The Seine passes through the city of Rouen where barges are moored along the river banks.

Beyond the city of Rouen, with its factories and docks along the riverside, the Seine is almost an artificial channel. The banks have been concreted and the water is dirty and oily, although the pretty Normandy countryside on either side gives a feeling of rural peacefulness.

When the Seine reaches its estuary, it is at its widest. Over the centuries its course has shifted back and forth in the estuary area, leaving flat, open areas of marshland. The north bank near Le Havre is now lined with refineries and factories but to the south is reclaimed marsh used for grazing.

11

The picturesque harbour at Honfleur. This once busy port in the Seine estuary is now reached by canal because the river has changed course and the harbour has silted up.

Farming in the Lower Seine

Above the chalk cliffs of the Lower Seine valley is open flat farmland where wheat and other cereals are grown, for example the plain of Caux. This area north of the Seine between Rouen and Le Havre stretches up to the English Channel and ends in white chalk cliffs dropping into the sea. Across the plain, trees have been planted to protect crops from the wind.

The river valleys of Normandy and the area around the Seine estuary are a lush green, with rich meadows due to the rain (over 750 mm every year) and moist warm air flowing in from the Atlantic. Apple orchards dot the countryside and the fields are grazed by brown-and-white Normandy cows. These cows are mostly reared for their rich milk, used in making cheese and butter – the region is famous for its dairy products.

Monsieur Martin

'I am checking and mending my nets after a night's fishing. I live in Honfleur, which has a sheltered harbour in the Seine estuary. It was once an important seaport – French explorers set sail to Canada from here. But the Seine has a mind of its own and it has gradually changed its course so that the entrance to Honfleur harbour has become silted up. Now the port is reached from the river along a specially built channel.'

Vernier Marshes

The Vernier Marshes lie in the estuary of the Seine and were once flooded with water. In the early seventeenth century, expert Dutch dyke builders (with their experience of low-lying marshland in Holland) were brought in to drain the area. Nowadays it is grazing land for cattle and horses. A lake that drains the marsh is home to many kinds of birdlife.

The European Community has tried to help the small farmers of Europe who, like many in France, own and manage their own farms and find it difficult to compete with big suppliers. As well as subsidies to the farmers, the European Community guarantees to keep the prices paid for milk, cereals and beef in particular, at a stable and high level. The community helps by buying up any extra crops the farmers produce that no-one wants to purchase. The area around the Seine valley is one of the main areas of Europe that has benefited from this system. When their livelihood is threatened, such as when cheap imports of meat come in from other countries, the French farmers are quick to defend themselves and are well-known for their public protests and demonstrations.

A tranquil scene in the Seine valley in Normandy.

Facts and figures about the River Seine

Length: 776 km. The third longest French river. Distance from source to sea as the crow flies is about 400 km.
Height at source: 471 m above sea-level.
Journey: The river passes through the regions of Burgundy, Champagne, Île de France and Normandy.
Drainage basin: 77,767 sq km (compare with Amazon 7,045,000 sq km and Rhine 224,000 sq km.)
Main tributaries: Rivers Aube, Yonne, Marne, Oise, Eure
Rate of flow: this varies between 365 m³/sec to 2,500 m³/sec.

3. HIGHWAY OF FRANCE

The French emperor Napoleon summed up the importance of the Seine as a traffic route when he said, 'Le Havre, Rouen and Paris are but a single town of which the Seine is the main street.' The Seine's gentle flow makes it an ideal waterway for boats and it has served as one for centuries.

About 2,500 years ago, Bronze Age people needed tin because it was a vital ingredient in making the metal bronze.

One of the main sources of European tin was Cornwall in England. After it had been brought across the English Channel, the tin had to be taken through France to the heart of Europe. Rivers were the only easy route through the densely wooded country of northern Europe and so the Seine became a major thoroughfare and trade route. Where the Seine became too shallow for navigation, everything was carried overland to the

The Seine has always been an important European waterway and is still used for transporting goods today. These barges are travelling between Rouen and Paris.

next river. This route is sometimes known as the Tin Road.

The Seine continues to be used for transporting goods. Its traffic increased enormously during the industrial revolution in the nineteenth century, when canals were either built or improved giving barges access to waterways all over Europe.

From its tributaries, such as the River Oise, barges can reach northern France and Belgium, and along the Marne and its canals, the Rhine and Germany. The Seine is the most westerly point where boats can enter the European canal system, allowing them to travel from Le Havre on the English Channel into the heart of Europe. A canal linking the Rhine with the Danube, completed at the end of 1992, enables barges to travel even as far as Eastern Europe and the Black Sea. The map shows how these waterways all link up.

Le Mascaret
Until the twentieth century, whenever there were high tides and the river was in flood, a bore or tidal wave used to race up the Seine from the estuary. Sea water rushing in would be trapped between the river banks and a giant wave would surge upstream, often full of mud. Called *Le Mascaret*, it used to wreck ships, cause all sorts of damage on shore and occasionally drown people. Tourists used to come and watch the wave as it passed. *Le Mascaret* no longer occurs because engineers have made changes to the channel in the Seine estuary and engineering works to the river banks.

Modern river traffic

The Lower Seine's channel is deep enough to allow ocean-going ships to travel from the sea as far as Rouen. About twelve of these enormous vessels

Canals and rivers link the River Seine to Europe's major waterways.

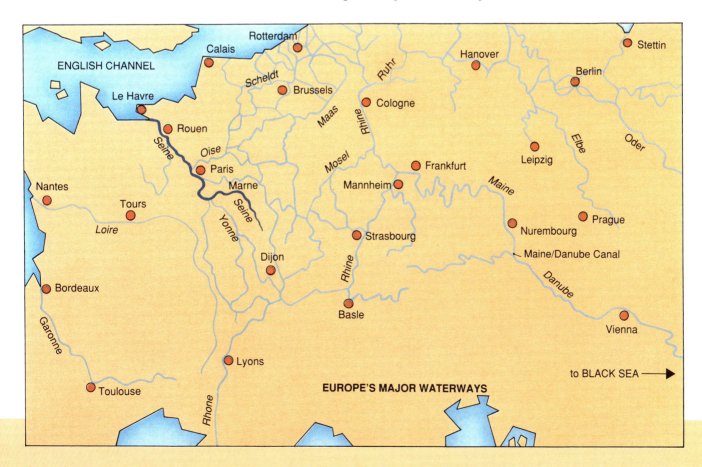

EUROPE'S MAJOR WATERWAYS

An ocean-going ship passes under the Tancarville Bridge on its way upriver to the port of Rouen.

move slowly through the rural landscape every day, towering above the apple-trees and cottages of the Normandy countryside. At Rouen, ships are loaded with goods for export or their imported cargo is unloaded. Some goods are transferred to barges to be taken further upstream, where the Seine is shallower and narrower and only suitable for smaller boats.

The busiest part of the Seine is this lower stretch, between Paris and the sea where the river passes the industrial areas of Paris, Rouen and Le Havre. Upstream from Paris the Seine is quieter because barge traffic for Europe turns off and uses the Oise and Marne Rivers. The Yonne meets the Seine at Montereau and provides a route for barges going to southern France and the Mediterranean.

Madame Roux

'My husband and I own this barge. We're moored up at Conflans-Sainte-Honorine for a few hours. Our work takes us up and down the Seine, often travelling along canals as far as Germany. We usually carry cargoes like sand, gravel or coal. Our car sits on the deck when we are travelling and we can swing it off the boat using a small crane. We live on our boat all the time, even though we have a house near the River Oise. I can't imagine life away from the river.'

Huge container ships sail along the Seine through the quiet Normandy countryside.

Beyond this junction only one or two barges are to be seen, travelling to Nogent where cereals are loaded. The Seine becomes a dead end for boats shortly afterwards.

Bargees, as the people who run barges are called, travel huge distances. One trip may mean going from Le Havre all the way through to Germany, a journey that will take many days. Some own their barges but others work for large organizations such as oil companies or sand and gravel extractors. Most boats are 400 tonne black steel barges, between 40 and 80 metres long and between 5 and 11 metres wide.

A common sight now on the Seine are the *pousseurs,* which are short but powerful tugs (only about 25 m long). Their strong engines can push several barges locked together. The number of barges they can handle is usually limited not by their power but by the size of the locks on the river.

Barges are floating homes, with all the comforts you might expect in a modern house. Many bargees have a car that sits on the deck and can be swung out on to the quayside with a small crane when they want to use it. In front of the living area is the huge metal cargo hold which is as big as a spacious hall inside.

Because bargees do not know where they will be from one week to the next – their home is wherever the next harbour is – children may have to be sent away to school. Quite a few bargees do own a house as well, where they may retire when they are older. But more often than not they cannot bear to be parted from their beloved river and there are places, such as Conflans-Sainte-Honorine, where retired bargees live in their boats moored to the riverbank.

There are several refuelling and servicing points along the Seine for barges but Conflans-Sainte-Honorine is often thought of as the waterway capital of the Seine. The waterfront is always crowded with barges. There are fuel stations and repair shops here as well as shops and cafés by the river where bargees can shop or gather to talk.

River transport is much less than it used to be and many barges are idle because of the lack of cargo. 85 per cent of goods in the European Community are now carried by road and rail because they are much quicker. Lorries can take goods direct to a customer without loading and unloading from a boat before final delivery.

Barges are most useful for carrying heavy and bulky goods that can be delivered directly to or collected from a factory, in particular raw materials such as coal, oil or sand and gravel. Most barge traffic on the Seine carries these types of cargoes. An oil pipeline from Le Havre to Paris has been built but this has not stopped barges carrying oil, because certain types of oil are not suitable for transporting along the pipeline and must be taken by boat.

Barges, carrying sand and gravel moor at Conflans-Sainte-Honorine, where the River Oise meets the Seine. This is an important refuelling and shopping stop for barges on the Lower Seine.

Making the Seine navigable

Although the Seine has natural features that make it a good waterway, it has needed a lot of work, particularly on the lower stretch, to make it navigable for today's ships. One of the biggest problems in the past was the way the river channel frequently shifted at the Seine's mouth near Le Havre. Mud and sandbanks appeared unexpectedly – for example between 1830 and 1852, 105 vessels ran aground near Quillebeuf alone, because of changes in the channel.

In 1887 the 25 km-long Tancarville Canal was built (shown on the map on page 33) which allows barges to reach Le Havre without using the estuary. But the most important work was done in the last thirty years, when a permanent channel in the mouth of the estuary was created by building dykes. These were extended underwater towards the sea and the channel between them deepened. Further upstream, as far as Rouen, the river is kept in place by concrete riverbanks and is regularly dredged.

Dredgers work constantly on the Lower Seine, keeping the river deep enough for the huge ships that sail along this stretch of the river.

The wide river winds towards its mouth at the sea. On the right, the Tancarville Canal cuts across the estuary marshes for 25 km towards the port of Le Havre.

Even with all these improvements, ships still need to be guided through the channel. Experienced river pilots are usually taken on board to help. The river up to Rouen is quite narrow, given the size of the ships, and lights mark the river banks on both sides for night sailing. Fog horns boom across the water when mist makes it impossible to see. Ships too have to take account of the tides — for example, if they travel from Rouen to the sea, they wait until the high tide has just turned and use it to help them downriver.

In order to make the Seine a reliable waterway for boats upstream of Rouen, locks and dams had to be built along much of its length. They control the flow and level of water in the river so keeping it constantly deep enough for the large barges. Higher up the river more locks had to be built. Between the highest point barges can reach (Marcilly) and Paris there are 19 locks – the river falls about 40 m in height along this stretch. From Paris down to Amfreville only 9 locks are needed because the river drops much less and is calmer and deeper.

Crossing the River

Building bridges across the Lower Seine is difficult because the river is so wide and because such huge ships use its waters. Until 1959 there was no bridge spanning the river between Le Havre and Rouen, a distance of about 130 km. The only way to cross was by ferry. The first bridge to be built was the Tancarville Bridge, still one of the largest suspension bridges in Europe. In 1977 another was built near Caudebec, the Brotonne Bridge.

Now a massive new bridge, the Pont de Normandie, is under construction not far from Le Havre. This will provide a link across the Seine estuary to the industrial area east of Le Havre. At other points along the Lower Seine small car ferries called *bacs* ply back and forward all through the day. Above Rouen where the river narrows and the traffic is nothing bigger than barges, bridges cross the Seine frequently. There are no tunnels anywhere under the Seine.

The massive Tancarville Bridge soars over the Seine, not far from its estuary. Downstream an even larger bridge is being built.

4. THE SEINE IN HISTORY

Celts to Vikings

On the upper reaches of the Seine, in a grave dating from the sixth century BC, the remains of a woman and her gold jewellery were found. Buried with this Celtic princess was a gigantic bronze vase, standing taller than a human being. This vase, called the Vase of Vix, is decorated with Greek battle scenes and was probably brought by cart hundreds of kilometres across Europe from Greece.

The site of this Celtic settlement where the treasure was found, Mont Lassois near Châtillon-sur-Seine, lay on the route of the ancient Tin Road and was probably a point at which Mediterranean merchants exchanged their products for the tin of Great Britain. The Celts (called Gauls in France by the Romans) settled at many points along the Seine valley but in 58 BC the invading Romans began to take over their lands.

As in most other parts of Europe, the Romans set up new towns such as Rotomagus, on the site of present-day Rouen; Lillebonne on the Seine estuary became a Roman capital and an important port.

Christianity spread through northern France and by the sixth century AD monasteries and abbeys that had been built along the banks of the Lower Seine had become cultural and economic centres. During this period, France was attacked and changed rulers several

The remains of a Roman amphitheatre at Lillebonne, near the mouth of the Seine.

The abbey of Jumièges in Normandy, originally founded in the seventh century, was later destroyed by the Vikings. This building was built in the tenth and eleventh centuries. In the Middle Ages the abbeys of the Seine valley were important centres of learning and culture.

times. The most important invaders were the Franks, who were a tribe from lands in eastern Europe. From his capital in France, the Frankish ruler King Charlemagne founded an enormous empire stretching across Europe in about AD 800. However, warrior Vikings were coming from the north.

Vikings and Normans

The rich valley of the Seine and its towns were an open invitation for the plundering Vikings. By AD 820 they were laying waste to the Lower Seine valley and by AD 885 Paris was under siege. But the riches began to run out, and within

A scene from the Bayeux Tapestry showing William of Normandy's men building the ships which they sailed across the Channel to invade England in 1066.

less then a century these savage pirates had settled down and turned into a creative civilization. The Vikings adopted Christianity and from church-burners they became abbey-builders. The Seine valley is one of the few places where the Vikings became a peaceful people.

In 911 the Viking leader Rollo signed a treaty with the king of France and was given the title of First Duke of Normandy. Normandy became an independent state. About a hundred years later, his descendant, William of Normandy, set his sights on the throne of England. His successful invasion in 1066 made him King of England as well as controlling a large part of northern France. From then on the kings of England felt they had a right to that part of France and the history of the two countries became intertwined.

The French wanted to bring Normandy under their rule and by 1202 King John of England had lost all his Norman lands to them (he was known as John Lackland because of this). In the mid-1300s, the English king Edward III tried to get them back and so began a long war between France and England, known as the Hundred Years' War. It was not until 1453 that the French finally regained Normandy and the Lower Seine valley.

Jeanne d'Arc
During the Hundred Years' War the English occupied Normandy. Jeanne d'Arc (known in Britain as Joan of Arc) encouraged and led the French people in defying the English, defeating them at Orléans in 1429. But she was captured and in 1431, after being tried and tortured, she was burned alive at the stake in the centre of Rouen by the English. Her heart, which did not burn, was thrown into the Seine. After the French recaptured Rouen, she was declared a heroine and later became the Patron Saint of France.

The Palace of Fontainebleau was lived in by French rulers from about 1500. The palace was decorated by famous artists and contained beautiful collections of paintings, sculptures and furniture.

France as one country

For about the next three hundred years France had a series of kings who ruled the land from palaces they built by the Seine. Some, like Louis XIV, (nicknamed the Sun King), encouraged artists, writers, painters, sculptors and architects and they produced great works which survive to this day. Versailles, started in 1661, is one of Louis XIV's most famous palaces, but he actually preferred to spend time at his smaller palace at Marly. This had a less formal atmosphere and lay on a peaceful wooded hillside directly overlooking the river.

The extravagant lifestyle of the kings of France and the poverty of the ordinary people finally brought about revolution. In 1789 the king was overthrown and the French Republic was born. It was not to last because within a few years Napoleon Bonaparte, a heroic French general, seized power and in 1804 declared himself emperor.

Napoleon took over the great palaces beside the Seine at St Cloud, Fontainebleau and the Tuileries. His favourite home was the beautiful palace of Malmaison where his wife Josephine loved to throw elegant parties.

The slender spire of Rouen Cathedral, dating from the thirteenth century, soars above the streets of the city. The cathedral was badly damaged during the Second World War (1939-45) but has now been restored.

In the last hundred years or so, the Seine valley has seen a great deal of war and destruction. In 1870 the Germans invaded France (the Franco-Prussian War) and then again there was fighting during the First and Second World Wars of 1914-18 and 1939-45. Many of the great historical cities, particularly Rouen, suffered terrible damage from bombing. Air attacks and ground fighting were concentrated in the Seine area, not only because of its importance as a route but also because it is home to the capital of France, Paris.

5. PARIS

Paris is not only the capital of France in name but it is the heart of the country's culture, fashion, commerce and industry. In a way that few other capital cities do, Paris leads and dominates France.

The first Parisians were the Parisii, Celtic settlers who set up a fishing village on an island in the Seine. The settlement lay at the best point for fording the river. Paris grew under Roman rule because it lay near where the Seine met the Oise and Marne rivers, an important trade junction. But it did not become a capital until AD 508 when Clovis, one of the Frankish invaders, decided Paris would be the town from which he would rule his new kingdom.

The famous waterfront

Along the banks of the Seine in Paris lie 13 km of some of the most famous river frontage in the world, lined with beautiful and historic buildings. The river curves through Paris forming two islands (the Île de la Cité and the Île Saint-Louis) and dividing Paris into two parts, the 'rive gauche' and the 'rive droite' (the left bank and the right bank). Numerous bridges cross the Seine; the Pont Neuf is the oldest (built in 1578) even though the name means new bridge.

The Île de la Cité was where the Parisii first settled and today it is the

The Pont Neuf spans the Seine, linking the Île de la Cité with both river banks.

point from which all distances from Paris are measured. In 1163 the great cathedral of Notre Dame was begun on the island, constructed in the soaring Gothic style of that time. It has managed to survive all the troubles of revolution and war. Not far away, on the *rive droite*, lies the Louvre, originally a royal palace but little lived in and now one of the most famous museums and art galleries in the world. Inside hangs the painting *Mona Lisa* by Leonardo da Vinci, among many other great works of art.

Away from the river are other well-known sights such as the white church of Sacré-Coeur in Montmartre, which used to be a quiet village on a hill. It attracted poets and artists and gradually became part of the city. The longest straight city street in France, the Champs-Élysées, runs from the Place de la Concorde and passes under the Arc de Triomphe, a memorial arch built to celebrate the victories of the Emperor Napoleon.

Nearly four kilometres beyond the Arc de Triomphe, on the other side of the Seine, the street ends at the modern financial and commercial quarter of Paris called La Défense.

Just as the Seine originally created Paris, so the Parisians now enjoy their river. People stroll along its banks with their wide pavements, browsing among second-hand book stalls. Others sit in cafés along the romantic riverside sipping wine or coffee. Along the river cruise glass-topped *bateaux-mouches*. These are tourist boats with windows all round, giving views of the famous sights.

Paris is a busy commercial and industrial city and the Seine also has to provide water and transport for businesses. The outskirts of the city have vast areas of docks and Paris is the largest inland port in France. A lot of commercial traffic uses the St. Denis and Ourcq canals which weave through the city skirting to the north of the Seine.

The Île de la Cité is home to one of the most famous landmarks of Paris, the Cathedral of Notre Dame. The cathedral was built in the twelfth century.

Left *On a hill overlooking the city centre lies Montmartre, crowned by the white domes and turrets of the Church of Sacré-Coeur.*

Right *Parisians enjoy the pavement cafes on the Champs-Élysées. In the distance is the Arc de Triomphe, built to celebrate Napoleon's victories.*

At night the Eiffel Tower is lit up and the river reflects the lights of Paris.

A growing city

The strength of Paris as an economic centre has attracted people from all over France and countries abroad. No other city in France provides such good opportunities and wages. The Paris region has about a quarter of the country's industry and 20 per cent of the population lives here. Sometimes people say Paris is so powerful that the rest of France seems like a desert by comparison.

The city used to be enclosed by walls but its edge is now defined by the Périphérique, a 3-lane expressway. However the built-up area extends far beyond this road.

After the last city walls were pulled down in 1919, the modern city began to spread out along the main roads. It was an unplanned sprawl. In the 1970s, rather than let this continue, plans were drawn up to channel new urban growth along two corridors, the Seine and the Marne valleys. Part of the plan was to create five new towns around Paris. Here new houses, shopping areas and modern recreational facilities were built, often with futuristic architecture and designs. Fast roads and rail systems link the new towns with central Paris.

In the inner city, parts have been pulled down to create modern buildings. The old fruit and vegetable market was moved to a site outside the centre in the 1970s and the old buildings were redeveloped to create the fashionable shopping area of Forum des Halles and the Pompidou Centre for Art and Culture.

Despite these developments, Paris continues to have problems like any large European city. As well as traffic congestion, more serious difficulties face the old suburbs of the city. The people who live there are mainly poor and unskilled, and most are foreigners. Large numbers from poorer European countries and North Africa came to live in France, hoping for a better life. Now there are over four million, the largest groups being the Portuguese, Algerians and Moroccans. Many end up living in slums unable to afford good housing.

6. SETTLEMENTS AND INDUSTRY

Although Paris and its surrounding new towns make up the largest settlement in the Seine valley, there are of course other towns which have grown up alongside the Seine. Le Havre and Rouen, both industrial towns and major ports, are two of the most important.

Rouen

Despite being so far inland, Rouen is one of France's main seaports because, as described in chapter 3, the river has been made navigable for large ships. Docks and cranes line the banks of the Seine for several kilometres west of Rouen and here the sea-going ships can dock and load and offload their cargoes.

Rouen was founded by the Romans at the first point they found it possible to build a bridge across the Seine. The Normans chose Rouen as their capital and for a time it fell under English rule when Henry V captured it during the Hundred Years' War. The city still has many old medieval quarters even though it was badly bombed during the Second World War. Afterwards large parts of Rouen were rebuilt and new factories sprouted up around the city. Today, when the wind blows in the wrong direction, smoke and the smell of chemical pollution hangs over the city.

Rouen has the advantage of being close to Paris, giving its industries a large market and also easy access to goods from the capital. It exports more abroad than any other French port, especially agricultural produce. Two important industries which use the Seine for transporting bulky raw materials are the paper and cereal processing industries. Other freight shipped in and out of Rouen includes chemicals, fertilizers, coal and products made from oil.

This sixteenth-century clock, is a famous sight in the old city of Rouen.

Le Havre

'Havre' means harbour but Le Havre did not become one until 1517 when it was built to replace the nearby port of Harfleur, which silted up as the Seine shifted its position in the estuary. Le Havre was used as a base for the long Atlantic crossings in the early days of the exploration of Canada, but its importance as a commercial port grew during the War of American Independence (1775-83). With war between England and its American colonies, most American products (such as tobacco and cotton) were shipped to Le Havre and from there distributed to their European markets.

Le Havre suffered even worse bombing than Rouen during the Second World War and was the most damaged port in the whole of Europe. In rebuilding the city, architects planned wide open spaces and filled them with modern concrete buildings.

The city has used its location at the mouth of the Seine and on the Channel coast to develop into France's second largest port. The dock areas have been continually improved and expanded, and are now a maze of water-filled basins able to take huge ocean-going tankers. Le Havre handles more container traffic than any other port in France and has one of the biggest locks in the world. This allows ships from the outer tidal basins

An ocean-going ship waits to be loaded at the docks in Rouen.

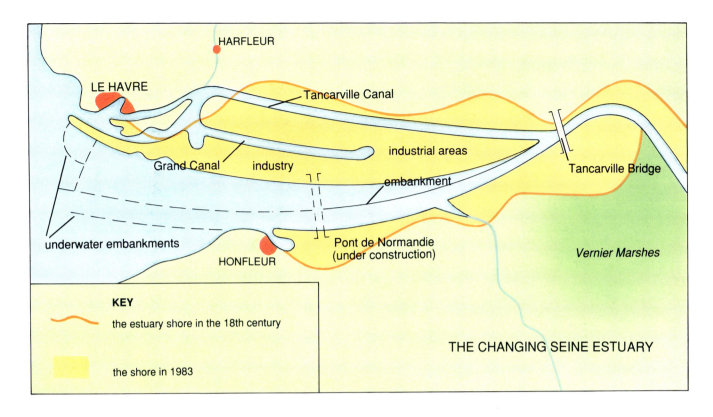

KEY

the estuary shore in the 18th century

the shore in 1983

HARFLEUR

LE HAVRE

Tancarville Canal

industrial areas

Grand Canal   industry

embankment

Tancarville Bridge

underwater embankments

HONFLEUR

Pont de Normandie
(under construction)

Vernier Marshes

THE CHANGING SEINE ESTUARY

The Seine estuary showing the changing shoreline during three hundred years.

through into the inner basins where the water level is kept constant so they can dock and unload easily.

The Lower Seine has been nicknamed the River of Petrol because so much oil is shipped along the river. The majority of France's imported oil arrives here in Le Havre and therefore oil refineries and other industries which use oil (for example, petro-chemical industries) have naturally been built nearby. On flat land stretching 20 km from Le Havre along the north bank of the Seine there is a mass of pipes, chimneys, tanks and new industrial buildings. Europe's biggest power station feeds the area with electricity generated from coal and oil brought in by ship.

Operating the port of Le Havre

At the entrance to the port of Le Havre is a 52 metre high tower with radio communications from which all shipping can be watched and all movements co-ordinated. The tugs at Le Havre are called *abeilles* (which means bees), and they buzz around the harbour bringing the large ships in and out. The port can take up to 250,000 tonne ships, but since the largest supertankers now go up to 500,000 tonnes, a new deep water port has had to be built further up the coast (the Antifer terminal).

The ancient centre of Troyes, a busy market town on the Upper Seine. The town still contains many medieval streets and houses.

Troyes

Towns like Troyes along the Upper Seine, east of the Île de France, are smaller than those between Paris and the sea. The Seine is no longer navigable for large barges and most settlements just serve the farmland around.

Troyes used to be an ancient crossroads and the capital of the Champagne region of France. The upland area where the Seine rises was once famed for its sheep, and a clothing industry grew up in Troyes which still survives. It is also a busy market town for the region.

Other industries of the Seine valley

The Lower Seine is not only well-known for its oil refineries and associated industries but also, moving closer to Paris, for its many car works. The region produces over two-thirds of all cars made in France and every big car manufacturer, such as Renault, Citroen and Peugeot, has at least one factory in the Seine valley. From Paris out to the town of Mantes-la-Jolie, there are many hectares of land along the banks of the Seine given over to car production. The river as well as rail is used for transporting cars and Le Havre is the chief car exporting port of France.

Left *The huge Port Jerome oil refinery lies on the banks of the Seine near the estuary of the river.*

Right *Rows of cars at a huge Renault factory not far from Mantes-la-Jolie, lie waiting for delivery for sale.*

Nuclear power

France produces most of the electricity it needs from nuclear power because the country has few coal or oil resources from which it can produce electricity. This power station at Nogent-sur-Seine uses water from the Seine. The nuclear reactor produces heat which turns the water to steam and this drives the electric generators. A lot of water is needed to produce the steam and so nuclear power stations are often built beside rivers or the sea.

As on many rivers throughout the world, sand and gravel extraction is a big business and there are many places along the Seine where pits are dug. Huge amounts of sand and gravel are needed for construction, both for buildings and for roads. An important source is the area around a river where it has deposited fine silt (often sand) or small stones (used for gravel). Companies buy the land or agree to use it for a time while they dig out what they need.

Since the Seine valley has so much industry, vast amounts of power are needed to keep it operating. Most power stations use coal and oil as fuel to make electricity, but this is very expensive because France has very few coal or oil supplies of its own. Nearly all is imported. As a result, France has had to find alternatives and has been one of the foremost countries in the world to develop nuclear power. There are now 56 nuclear power stations in France.

7. ART AND CULTURE

Claude Monet painted this picture of the harbour at Le Havre in 1872. He called his painting Impression: Sunrise. *It was this picture that gave the Impressionist painters their name.*

The Seine is probably the most painted river in the world. It inspired some of the greatest French artists, in particular the group known as the Impressionists, who lived during the latter part of the nineteenth century.

The Impressionists studied light and colour, painting natural scenes such as landscapes and informal groups of people. In the mid-1800s this was not considered good painting and was frowned upon; people preferred artists to

This view of the River Seine was painted by the Impressionist artist Alfred Sisley.

paint traditional subjects such as realistic portraits and pictures of battles or imaginary scenes from classical stories. It was also unusual at that time to paint outdoors and not in a studio. Artists began to challenge these traditions, at first gathering in the village of Barbizon in the Forest of Fontainbleau.

In 1874 a group of them put together an exhibition of their paintings. It included pictures by artists such as Monet, Renoir, Pissarro, Sisley and Degas. The critics laughed at them and called the artists 'Impressionists', as a term of abuse. But as time passed, the skill and beauty of their paintings began to be recognized.

Claude Monet

Claude Monet is probably the most famous of the French Impressionist painters and he is one of the movement's first and finest artists. Early on in his career he refused to study old classical works, preferring to experiment with painting on the streets of Paris. He was particularly interested in the way light and colour worked together. From about 1870, he painted beside the Seine at Argenteuil, often in the company of other Impressionists. Later he moved to Giverny where he painted many pictures of his garden including his famous water-lily paintings.

One series of paintings Monet made was of Rouen Cathedral (right), which he painted over thirty times from every angle, every hour of the day in every light, capturing the pattern of light and shadow on its walls.

For about ten years the Impressionist artists spent much of their time around the village of Argenteuil, on the Seine. They painted the countryside, the streets, the river, the people and each other, almost always out of doors, trying to capture the colours and changing light. The painters Pissarro and Cézanne worked nearby at Pontoise.

The Impressionists chose the area because it was close to Paris and also because of the light in the Seine valley with its gentle skies, soft shadows and colours under the watery sun. The wide and slow river was sometimes rippling and sometimes like glass, but it always had the reflections of the sky, boats and trees.

Monet often painted this lily-pond, which he created in his garden at Giverny.

8. PLEASURES OF THE SEINE

Food and drink

The people of the Seine valley enjoy their food and treat it as one of the main pleasures of life, as do all the French. Here in the north of France, dairy products such as butter, cream and cheese are important ingredients in French cooking.

Many varieties of cheese are made in the Seine valley area, some of which are now exported abroad and have become world famous. From Normandy comes the square, brown and creamy Pont l'Évêque cheese, the farmhouse Neufchâtel and the soft and rather smelly Livarot. These have been made since the thirteenth century. The better

Above *A cider festival in Normandy, where cider apples are grown; and* **left** *fish and shellfish for sale on the quay at Honfleur.*

known Camembert cheese is actually quite recent, invented in the nineteenth century on a Normandy farm. Nowadays Camembert is made in factories all over France.

From an area near the Seine to the south-east of Paris, comes the cheese called Brie. There are several different kinds, all eaten in segments from a large disc. French people say that Brie is good for the health because it replaces important bacteria in the stomach.

Dishes in Normandy use birds such as duck, grouse, pheasant and partridge, and a huge variety of fish and shellfish are caught in the sea near Le Havre. Restaurants inland as far as Paris quite often have fresh mussels, lobster, crab, oysters, shrimps and cockles on their menus.

Monsieur Lenoir

'I am a cheese-seller' and I come every Sunday to this riverside street market to sell my cheeses. I am cutting a Brie, which as you can see, is a round white cheese. It has a soft crust on the outside and should be creamy inside. It takes about 145 litres of milk to make one Brie de Melun and a good cheese will be kept in a cellar for two months to mature. Mass-produced Brie is only left for about ten days before it is packed to be sold. I only sell good cheese!

France is one of the great wine producers of Europe, and the Seine valley makes a contribution. As we have seen in chapter 2, the Upper Seine lies within the area where champagne grapes are grown. A wine is only allowed to use the name champagne if it is made from particular types of grape grown in certain areas of the province of Champagne.

The area around the Seine attracts visitors from all over the world, who come to see historic buildings like Vaux-le-Vicomte Chateau, built in 1656.

Anglers beside the Seine in Normandy. Behind are the remains of an old bridge that once crossed the river.

Leisure on the Seine

The Seine is not just a useful highway but is in many places a beautiful river and valley which people enjoy for its own sake. As well as the natural beauty of the area, there are castles, abbeys and historic towns which tourists come from all over the world to see.

The river itself is a playground for people who like boats – motor boats, sailing boats, rowing boats and canoes all use the river. Abandoned gravel pits beside the Seine are filled with water and become ideal lakes for water sports like windsurfing and waterskiing. Some pits too have been landscaped to provide parks, picnic areas and camping grounds.

The banks of the Seine and its tributaries and canals are always lined with anglers, especially at weekends. Downstream from Rouen fewer people care to fish because of river pollution. In the countryside around the Seine, the French enjoy *la chasse*, shooting and hunting mostly for game birds. Hunting was a favourite sport of the French kings and this is the main reason why the woods along the banks of the Seine, where they hunted deer and boar, have remained largely untouched over the centuries.

Cycling is the national sport and the roads around the Seine valley have their share of French cyclists. Other people like to ride horses through the woods and countryside. On the Normandy coast in summer holiday-makers sunbathe on the beaches and swim. Near the mouth of the Seine is the town of Deauville, a luxury resort with casinos, pools and race courses, attracting the rich and famous from many countries.

A large park, the Brotonne Regional Nature Park, has been created to protect the natural scenery in part of the Lower Seine valley. It has nature trails and information to teach visitors about the countryside and natural life in the area. The Seine valley is also home to other kinds of park – amusement parks. Near the new town Cergy-Pontoise is Mirapolis, a theme park with hectares of leisure activities like roller-coasters and displays for children. On the other side of Paris, near the new town of Marne-la-Vallée, is Euro Disneyworld.

Hunters with their guns and dogs enjoy la chasse *(shooting game birds), at weekends.*

9. LOOKING TO THE FUTURE

Water control

Few rivers flow regularly throughout the year. Although the Seine is one of the world's more gentle rivers, its flow too varies enough to cause problems.

There are two risks during the year. First, there is the threat of flooding in winter and spring when rainfall is heaviest. Flooding can be serious in Paris because there are so many people and buildings. Second, in summer and autumn there is the possibility of water shortages which affect farming and industry, as well as boats using the river. In order to prevent either of these happening, work has been done to try to regulate and control the Seine.

Half the water that reaches Paris comes from the Yonne tributary and so this was seen as the most important place to start; a dam was built there in 1950. Since then, dams have also been built on the Marne and on the Seine. Near Troyes a system of balancing lakes and canals diverts and puts water back into the Seine as and when needed. Although the flood risk has been reduced, the lakes have not proved as useful as expected in controlling the Seine because they are too far upstream. The Seine is still a small river at this point and many more tributaries add water below Troyes. Efforts are being made to find a suitable site on the Yonne for another dam or barrier.

Pollution problems

The Seine is not the most polluted river in Europe but like any other river in an industrialized country it is certainly not clean. The worst pollution is on the Lower Seine, after the river has passed

Poses Dam controls the waters of the Seine. On the right are locks and in the foreground is a device for measuring the temperature of the water.

Left *This canal feeds surplus water from the Seine into nearby lakes, controlling the flow of the river so that it does not flood.*

Right *The Seine has many uses, not only for pleasure and sport but also for transport and industry.*

through the industrial areas on the outskirts of Paris and the city of Rouen. Industry is the biggest source of pollution on the Seine; chemical factories, paper factories and oil refineries all discharge unused materials into the river. Added to this is oil from the barges, sewage from towns and agricultural fertilizer seeping through the soil into the river.

It is not only chemicals that cause pollution. One of the Seine's problems is thermal pollution, which means warming of the river. Power stations along the Seine's banks pour hot water they do not use into the river. If the temperature rises above a certain level, river life dies.

Different demands

The Seine flows through a heavily populated part of Europe and it is used by many people for different things. Not only does the river provide drinking water for the urban area of Paris but it also supplies water to factories and farms. As a transport route it is still a vital waterway for France. People use it too for recreation, enjoying the scenery of its valley and water sports on the river itself. In places the commercial use of the Seine clashes with people's enjoyment of the river. Somehow in the future a balance will have to be kept between all the different demands on this important French waterway.

45

GLOSSARY

Aqueduct A bridge with a channel for carrying water across a valley.

Bacteria Tiny organisms that are too small to be seen but are found everywhere. Some cause diseases.

Bayeux Tapestry A famous work of embroidery made in the 11th or 12th century showing the Norman conquest of England in 1066.

Bore A tidal wave of water that rushes up rivers.

Bronze Age A prehistoric age, about 3,000 to 4,000 years ago, when bronze was used to make tools and weapons.

Celts A people made up of many tribes who lived in Europe over 2,000 years ago.

Container traffic Transporting goods in large metal boxes. The boxes are of a standard size so they can easily fit on ships, trains or lorries.

Descendants The children, grandchildren, great-grandchildren and so on, of people who lived in earlier times.

Dredge To dig up mud or sand from the bottom of a river to make it deeper.

Dykes Banks made of earth or concrete.

Estuary The place where a river widens as it nears the sea. Rivers are usually tidal here.

European Community The group of twelve European countries working together to promote industry, agriculture and trade.

Extraction The process of digging or pulling something out.

Fertile Able to make things grow well.

Gothic A medieval style of architecture characterized by soaring spires, flying buttresses and tall windows. Many cathedrals and churches in France were built in the Gothic style.

Limestone A kind of rock formed millions of years ago mostly from the shells or skeletons of animals such as shellfish and corals.

Lock A section of a river or canal that can be closed off so that the water level can be raised or lowered.

Meander To follow a winding course. The word comes from the River Meander in Turkey.

Medieval Describes people or things from the Middle Ages.

Middle Ages The long period of European history from about AD 500 to AD 1400.

Navigable Describes a waterway which is wide, deep and safe enough for boats.

Nuclear power Power made when atoms are split. Nuclear power stations usually produce energy from splitting atoms of the mineral uranium.

Oil-seed rape A plant that produces oil. It is grown as a crop in fields.

Pilots People who guide ships, usually in and out of harbours.

Refineries Factories where raw materials, such as sugar and oil, are cleaned and purified.

Republic A country without a king or queen, usually with a president as head of state.

Silt Very fine particles of soil and rock carried by a river.

Source The place where a river starts.

Subsidies Money given, usually by a government, in order to help a group of people and their businesses.

Suburbs Districts surrounding the central areas of a large town or city.

Tidal Describes a river that rises and falls with the sea. It is usually only the lower part of a river near the sea that does this.

Tributary A river that runs into another larger one.

War of American Independence A war fought from 1775-83 between the North American colonies and Britain to gain independence for the colonies from British rule.

BOOKS TO READ AND FURTHER INFORMATION

There are few books specifically about the Seine. Look for books about France or Paris or one of the other subjects that interests you, for example, water transport or canals. Some guide books like the Michelin Green Guides to France have very useful general information about different areas.

Books for younger readers:
The Seine by C.A.R. Hills (Wayland, 1981)
Countries of the World: France by Alan Blackwood and Brigitte Chosson (Wayland, 1988)
People and Places: France by L. Bender (Macmillan 1988)
France: the Land and its People by Chantal Tunnacliffe (Macdonald, 1986)
Rivers by Terry Jennings (Oxford University Press, 1990)

For older readers:
Impressions of the Seine by Carey More and Julian More (Pavilion, 1991)
The Seine by Antony Glyn (Weidenfeld and Nicolson, 1966)
Article entitled 'The Seine' in *National Geographic* April 1982

Useful addresses
Musée Claude Monet, 27620, Giverny. (Can be reached by train from Gare St. Nazaire, Paris to Vernon.)
Musée de la Batellerie, Conflans-Sainte-Honorine.
Fine Arts Museums at Le Havre and Rouen.
Musée de la Marine de Seine, Rue de la Prison, 14600 Honfleur.
Louvre Museum, Paris.
Nogent-sur-Seine Nuclear Power Station – open to the public.

Picture acknowledgements
All photographs are by Julia Waterlow except the following: Bridgeman Art Library 37; Michael Holford 24; Tony Stone Worldwide /D. H. Endersbee cover,/Doug Armand 30,/Erika Craddock 28,/S. & N. Geary 29 (lower),/Bruno De Hogues 29 (upper). The map on page 5 is by Peter Bull and artwork on pages 15 and 33 by John Yates.

INDEX

numbers in **bold** relate to
illustrations

abbeys 22, 23, 42
Amfreville 10
architecture 39
Aube, River 7

bargees 17
barges 14, **14**, 16, 17, 18
bridges 21
　Brotonne Bridge 20
　Pont de Neuf 27, **27**
　Pont de Normandie 21
　Tancarville Bridge 16, 21,
　　21
Brotonne Regional Nature
　Park 43

canals 4, 25, 28, 45
car ferries 21
car production 35, **35**
cathedrals 4, 26, 28
Celts 22
champagne grapes 7, 41
Champagne region 7, 41
Charlemagne, Emperor 23
Châtillon-sur-Seine 6, 22
cheeses 40, 41
cider festival **40**
Conflans-Ste-Honorine 17,
　18, **18**
container ships 17

dairy products 12
dam 10, **10**, 44
dredgers 19
dykes 19

English Channel 11, 12
European canal system 15
European Community 15

farming 7
　oil-seed rape 8
　sugar beet 7, 8, 10
　wheat 7, 8, 12
flooding 44
Forest of Fontainbleau 9, 38

Giverny 38, 39, **39**
gravel pits 36, 42

Honfleur 12, **12**, 40

Île de France 8, 10
Impressionist painters 37-9,
　37
industries 25

Jeanne d'Arc 25

La Chasse 42, **43**
Le Havre 11, 12, 17, 31,
　32-3, **33**, 35
Le Mascaret 15
Lillebonne 22
literature 39
locks 19, **19**, 20, 32
Loing, River 7
Louis XIV, King 25

Marne, River 7, 16, 27
marsh 11
meanders 10
Monet, Claude **37**, 38, **39**
Montereau 16

Napoleon I, Emperor 14, 25
Normandy 11, 12, 13, 16, 40,
　43
nuclear power 36

ocean-going ships 15, 16, 32
oil refineries 33, **35**
Oise, River 7, 15, 16

Paris 4, 9, 10, 27-30
pollution 43, 44
Poses Dam 10, **44**
power station 33, 45

river pilots 20
Rollo, Duke 24
Roman ampitheatre **22**
Romans 7, 22
Rouen 10, 11, **11**, 12, 15, 16,
　20, 31, **31**, **32**

Seine, River
　course 4
　estuary 11, **33**
　flow 13
　source 4, 6, **6**
　transport 4, 14, **14**, 15, 16,
　　17, 18
　tributaries 7, 15

Tancarville Canal 19, 20

Vernier Marshes **13**
Vikings 4, 23, 24
vineyards 7

water control 44
William of Normandy 24

Yonne, River 7, 16